First Facts®

UNEXPLAINED MYSTERIES

The Unsolved Mystery of HAUNTED HOUSES

by Katherine Krohn

CAPSTONE PRESS
a capstone imprint

First Facts are published by Capstone Press,
1710 Roe Crest Drive, North Mankato, Minnesota 56003
www.capstonepub.com

Library of Congress Cataloging-in-Publication Data
Krohn, Katherine E.
The unsolved mystery of haunted houses / by Katherine Krohn.
    pages cm.—(First facts. Unexplained mysteries.)
Includes bibliographical references and index.
Summary: "Presents the mystery of haunted houses, including current theories and
famous examples"—Provided by publisher.
ISBN 978-1-4765-3097-0 (library binding)
ISBN 978-1-4765-3428-2 (eBook PDF)
ISBN 978-1-4765-3442-8 (paperback)
1. Haunted houses—Juvenile literature. 2. Ghosts—Juvenile literature. I. Title.
BF1475.K765 2014
133.1′22—dc23   2013003686

Editorial Credits
Anna Butzer, editor; Juliette Peters, designer; Wanda Winch, media researcher;
Kathy McColley, production specialist

Photo Credits
Alamy: Dale O'Dell, 19, The Marsden Archive, 11, Zuma Wire Service, 12; AP Images:
Journal Gazette/Kevin Kilhoffer, 14, *Times Daily*/Jim Hannon, 21; Corbis: Reuters/
Jessica Rinaldi, 16; Shutterstock: Doug Stacey, 8, Jeff Kinsey, 7, mmpriv, 4, sgrigor,
design background, Vinterriket, cover, zeber, design background

Printed in the United States of America in North Mankato, Minnesota.
032013   007223CGF13

Table of Contents

Chapter 1

A Spooky House

A door slams shut. Lights turn on and off. Could this house be **haunted**?

Strange events sometimes lead people to believe a house is haunted. They blame **ghosts**. Experienced ghost hunters can't always find what causes weird events inside houses.

haunted—having strange events happen often, possibly because of ghosts

ghost—a spirit of a dead person believed to haunt people or places

Many people say haunted houses are old, spooky, and empty. But some haunted houses are new and lived in. Other haunted houses are buildings where people work or visit. Some haunted houses are famous. People have told of strange events in the White House since the 1920s.

Ghost hunters say that only one out of 10 spooky houses has a ghost.

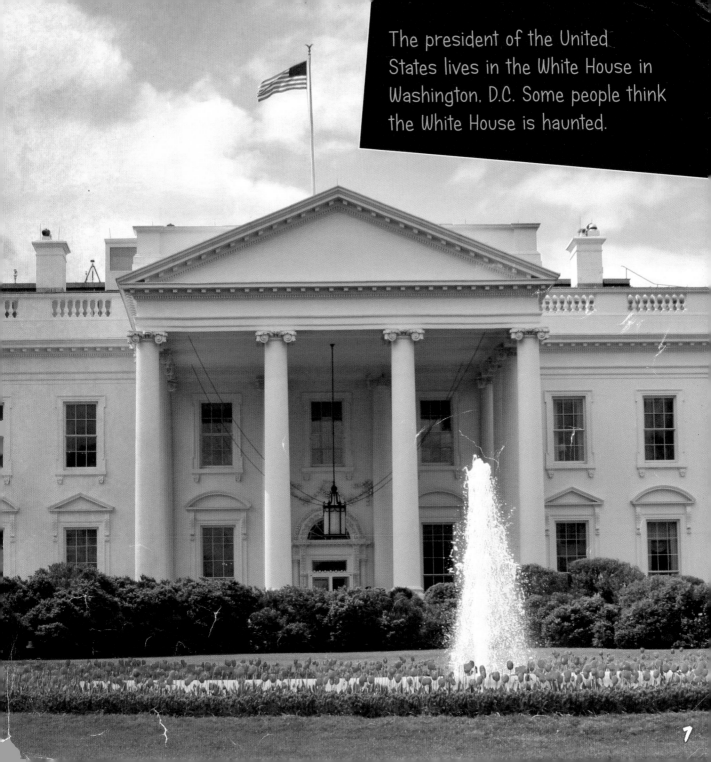

The president of the United States lives in the White House in Washington, D.C. Some people think the White House is haunted.

Edinburgh Castle was built
in 1130. People started telling
ghost stories about it a few
years later.

History and Legend

People have been telling stories about haunted houses for hundreds of years. Edinburgh Castle in Scotland has been the setting of many scary stories. In 1650 people said a ghost of a drummer boy appeared near the castle. People have also seen a ghostly dog near the castle.

Strange activity in Edinburgh Castle includes more than ghost sightings. Workers in the castle have heard pipe organ music coming from inside the walls.

The Borley **Rectory** was one of the most haunted houses in England. In the 1800s the family who lived there began to see creepy things. They said a woman's ghost walked through the rectory's garden. Writings also appeared on the walls. No one could explain how the writings got there.

rectory—a house or building where a church leader lives

A fire destroyed most of the Borley Rectory in 1938. The rest was torn down in 1944.

Chapter 3

Haunted or Not?

Most people try to stay far away from haunted houses. But ghost hunters try to find haunted houses. They look for **proof** that ghosts are there. They use cameras to record ghosts and objects moving on their own. They also use **thermometers** to find cold spots in a house. Some people believe ghosts take heat from a room.

proof—facts or evidence that something is true

thermometer—an object used to measure temperature

Some ghost hunters claim ghosts have a type of electric energy. Special meters measure this energy. Can ghost hunters prove ghosts are real with the meters?

True:
High energies have been recorded in areas where ghosts were reported.

False:
Electrical wires and microwaves can create high amounts of energy. Sometimes a building's bad wiring can cause the energy levels to be higher.

True:
In places with high-energy recordings, some people feel they are being watched.

False:
Sometimes people feel nervous or scared for no reason.

Some ghost hunters believe that a ghost can walk through a person. They believe this may make the person feel cold.

Ghost hunters use other tools to find ghostly noises in haunted houses. These tools include recorders. Sometimes recorders capture strange sounds believed to be ghosts. These recordings are called electronic voice phenomenons.

People have given many reasons for why ghosts haunt houses. Some people believe ghosts like to stay near the things they cared for.

ghost hunting equipment

True or False?

Can people really track ghosts with recorders?

True:
Ghost hunters often record strange noises in haunted houses.

False:
Wind or leaky pipes can make spooky sounds in houses. Many houses make noises during the winter. Cold weather can make floors creak.

True:
Some ghost hunters say they have recorded ghosts' voices.

False:
There's no proof that a ghost's voice can be recorded. Some people believe whispering into a microphone can sound like a ghost recording.

Ghost hunters knock on a door to see if there is a ghost behind it.

16

Ghost hunters usually search for **evidence** at night. They like to work when it is quiet. Ghost hunters often search for information in teams. Each person on the team has a different job. Ghost hunters spend a lot of time searching for clues in haunted houses. They spend even more time carefully looking at the information they gather.

evidence—information, items, and facts that help prove something to be true or false

Chapter 4

Searching for Answers

Many people believe ghosts haunt houses. Others say there is no real proof. They think the signs have natural causes or are **hoaxes**. Wind can blow through houses and make cold spots or shut doors. Bad wires can cause lights to turn on and off. Many times ghost hunters find natural reasons for the sights and sounds in houses.

hoax—a trick to make people believe something that is not true

Some people say this photo shows a ghost. Other people think it may be a hoax.

Thousands of people study haunted houses. Ghost hunters will continue to search for answers. Maybe someday they will prove ghosts are real. Until then, stories of haunted houses will continue to amaze and scare people.

Ghost hunters search for unexplained activity in an Alabama home in 2011.

Glossary

evidence (EV-uh-duhnss)—information, items, and facts that help prove something to be true or false

ghost (GOHST)—a spirit of a dead person believed to haunt people or places

haunted (HAWN-ted)—having strange events happen often, possibly because of ghosts

hoax (HOAKS)—a trick to make people believe something that is not true

proof (PROOF)—facts or evidence that something is true

rectory (REK-tuh-ree)—a house or building where a church leader lives

thermometer (thur-MOM-uh-tur)—an object used to measure temperature

Read More

Martin, Michael. *The Unsolved Mystery of Ghosts.* The Unexplained. North Mankato, Minn.: Capstone Press, 2013.

McCormick, Lisa Wade. *Haunted Houses: The Unsolved Mystery.* Mysteries of Science. Mankato, Minn.: Capstone Press, 2010.

Stone, Adam. *Haunted Houses.* The Unexplained. Minneapolis: Bellwether Media, Inc., 2011.

Internet Sites

FactHound offers a safe, fun way to find Internet sites related to this book. All of the sites on FactHound have been researched by our staff.

Here's all you do:

Visit *www.facthound.com*

Type in this code: 9781476530970

Super-cool stuff! Check out projects, games and lots more at
www.capstonekids.com

Index